Essential Question
What do good citizens do?

The Food Crew

by Jacqui Briggs
illustrated by Donald Wu

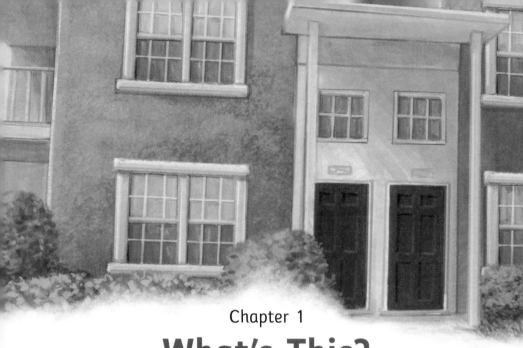

Chapter 1
What's This?

Sonja and Ben skipped down the city sidewalk toward home. Ben's older brother, Jason, walked with them. Jason was home from college.

Sonja said, "My mom said she'd have a snack for us after school."

"Great!" Ben said. "I'm starving!"

"My favorite after-school snack is bananas and crunchy peanut butter on toast. It's perfect with milk," said Sonja.

"What is your favorite after-school snack?" Sonja asked Ben.

"Mini pizzas," said Ben. "Jason takes flour tortillas and tops them with sauce, cheese, green peppers, and spices. Then he bakes them. They get nice and crispy."

"That sounds delicious! My mouth is watering!" Sonja turned to Jason. "Could you make that the next time I come over?" Sonja asked. Jason nodded.

Lakeland
Food Pantry

Inside, they rode the elevator. Jason followed as the two friends walked to Sonja's apartment.

"Hey, Sonja, what is that? Is it a present?" Ben asked. He pointed to a box outside of Sonja's door.

Sonja looked puzzled. "I don't know," she said slowly. "I've never seen it before. Maybe a neighbor left it for us."

"I wonder what is inside!" Ben said.

Ben and Sonja peered inside. "It's full of food! Maybe someone dropped off groceries for your family," said Ben.

"We can ask Mom," Sonja replied. "Hey, let's knock on the door and hide from her when she opens it!"

Chapter 2
Mom Explains

Sonja pressed the doorbell and hid with Ben. They could hear her mother's footsteps. Suddenly, the door opened. "Hello?" Sonja's mom called.

Sonja and Ben jumped out. "Surprise!"

Sonja's mom jumped. "You scared me!" she said. "Come inside. Your snack is ready." She waved good-bye to Jason. He would come back later to pick up Ben.

Sonja and Ben hungrily ate their snack. As she bit into an apple slice, Sonja asked, "Why is there food in that box in the hallway?"

"It is for the Lakeland Food Pantry," she explained. "The Lakeland Food Pantry has taken responsibility for collecting food. They made a promise to give this food to the needy."

"Who are the needy?" asked Ben.

"They are people who need something important, like food or shelter. They don't have enough food or a place to live," answered Sonja's mom.

"Are we needy?" asked Sonja.

"No, because we have what we need. We have a home, and we have plenty to eat," Sonja's mom explained.

"Why was the box by your door?" Ben asked curiously.

"It was there so we could donate food," Sonja's mom replied. "We can fill it with food we want to give to others. Today I went through our cupboards and picked some items to donate."

Sonja held up her carrot stick. "I want to be helpful! I can give my carrot stick."

"Actually, a can of carrots would be better," said Mom. "The food may stay in the pantry for a long time. It must be food that won't spoil. Fresh fruits and vegetables aren't good for donating."

"Let's see what else we can donate. Mom, can we check the cupboard again?" Sonja asked.

"Sure!" Mom said. "In fact, why don't you take a box to school? You could tell your class about hunger and collect food. You could help people."

Chapter 3
The Plan

The next day, Sonja and Ben talked to their class about hunger. "Everyone has the right to have enough food," said Sonja. "But many people in our city are hungry."

"Food pantries give food to those people," said Ben. "The Lakeland Food Pantry collects food for the needy. This box is for donations."

Ben and Sonja explained what kinds of food to donate. Then Sonja asked, "Ms. Lee, could we please collect donations in our class?"

"Of course," said Ms. Lee. "Hunger is an important issue. We should do something. Class, who wants to help?"

Everyone raised a hand. Ms. Lee counted the votes. Everyone really wanted to help.

"We could organize a school-wide food collection. I will talk to our principal," Ms. Lee said.

The next day, Ms. Lee had an announcement. "Good news! Principal Marshall has determined that a food drive is a great idea!" The class cheered.

"We will collect food items this week. Bring your canned and boxed food items to school. Place them in this box. On Friday, people from the Lakeland Food Pantry will come pick up the food," Ms. Lee said.

Later that week, a worker from the food pantry visited the class. "Thank you for your donations!" he said. "This food will help many people in our city. We brought special shirts to wear whenever you collect food. Wear them with pride. People like you are real champions!"

Everyone felt good.

Sonja and Ben were proud of their class. "It feels great to help others. I'm so glad we volunteered to collect food," Sonja said.

"I know! I can't believe how much we collected! It will help a lot of people," Ben said.

"I hope we can do a food drive every year!" Sonja replied.

Respond to Reading

Summarize

Use details to help you summarize *The Food Crew*.

Character	Clue	Point of View

Text Evidence

1. How do you know *The Food Crew* is realistic fiction?   Genre

2. How do Ben and Sonja feel when they first see the box?   Point of View

3. Figure out the meaning of *helpful* on page 9 using your knowledge of suffixes.   Suffixes

4. Write about how Ben and Sonja feel about the food drive.   Write About Reading

Compare Texts
Read about a real-life school that helps others by giving food.

A School Feeds Others

Recently, a school in New York decided to help a local food kitchen. Early in November, teachers, kids, and parents arrived at Tuxedo Park Elementary School. They came to bake Thanksgiving pies. They would give the pies to the Suffern Soup Kitchen.

The Suffern Soup Kitchen is in Suffern, New York. It provides food to people who don't have enough to eat.

That morning, everyone unpacked bags of groceries and supplies. They brought sour apples, butter, and apple peelers.

Helping others can be a lot of fun.

The kids were excited to help needy people. The pies would be served with turkey, mashed potatoes, and other delicious side dishes.

First, the kids and parents peeled apples. Then they cut the apples into slices. They put sugar and cinnamon on the apples and poured this filling into crusts. The teachers put the pies in the oven. Soon the school smelled great!

The kids decorated pie boxes while the pies baked. Once the pies cooled, they put the pies in the boxes. They made 57 pies in all. The teachers then delivered the pies to the Suffern Soup Kitchen. The soup kitchen was thankful to have the pies to serve. The people eating at the soup kitchen enjoyed the apple pies.

Helping with Hunger

The Suffern Soup Kitchen has helped feed the community for over 20 years. It serves dozens of people each day. It is open seven days a week, 365 days a year.

Make Connections

How are the kids at Tuxedo Park School good citizens? Essential Question

How are the kids at Tuxedo Park School like Ben and Sonja? Text to Text

Focus on
Social Studies

Purpose To learn about careers that involve helping others

Step I ▶ Think of jobs in which a person helps others. Choose a family member or school employee who does that job and interview him or her.

Step 2 ▶ Ask questions such as these:

1. How do you help others in your job?

2. What kind of training do you have to have for your job?

Step 3 ▶ Share what you learned with the class.